HUMBERT SUMMER

HUMBERT SUMMER

A.K.
BLAKEMORE

EYEWEAR PUBLISHING

First published in 2015
by Eyewear Publishing Ltd
74 Leith Mansions, Grantully Road
London W9 1LJ
United Kingdom

Typeset with graphic design by Edwin Smet
Cover photographs by Alice Zoo
Printed in England by TJ International Ltd, Padstow, Cornwall

The right of A.K. Blakemore to be identified as author of
this work has been asserted in accordance with section 77
of the Copyright, Designs and Patents Act 1988
ISBN 978-1-908998-41-5

WWW.EYEWEARPUBLISHING.COM

THE
MELITA HUME
POETRY PRIZE

A.K. Blakemore is the 2014 winner of the Melita Hume Poetry Prize. She received
£1,400 and this publication by Eyewear Publishing. The 2014 Judge was Emily Berry.
Her citation read:

A.K. Blakemore's collection *Humbert Summer* had my attention from the outset; the
more I returned to it, the more it hooked me in (and by the way, it has claws). This is a
book written in a rebellious spirit – playful, defiant, sure of itself – a burst of quickfire
poems delivering twisted despatches from modern life. Blakemore's voice is that of an
anti-heroine who isn't shy to show her hand – a hand that might have nails like 'bright
important spikes', contain 'chipped glass' or sometimes wield a knife. The poems seem to
speak for a generation bored of its idols, somehow turning disaffected youth's trademark
ennui into something altogether more celebratory. Bad dreams become good ones.
'know that i am serially unkind / to those that love me', the poet warns – it's worth the risk.

FOR
STEFFAN

A.K. BLAKEMORE

A.K. Blakemore was born in southeast London in 1991, and
read English Literature at St Edmund Hall, Oxford. She
was named a Foyle Young Poet of the Year twice, in 2007
and 2008. Her work has since been widely published and
anthologised, and was included in the 2009 Bloodaxe
anthology, *Voice Recognition: 21 Poets for the 21st Century*.
She has performed at the Secret Garden Party and Latitude
festivals, and at the Royal Albert Hall as part of the BBC's
Proms season. Her first pamphlet was released as part of
the Nasty Little Press *Nasty Little Intros* series in 2013. She
currently lives and works in south London.

Table of Contents

sick of the beats — 9
she's a star — 11
you can put it anywhere — 12
Humbert Summer — 13
indie — 14
glitch — 15
Valerie Solanas — 16
cat — 17
zygote — 18
the clitorids — 19
ars poetica — 20
autophilia — 21
Joshua — 22
Rick James — 23
fashion week — 25
hate — 26
Ross and Rachel… — 27
magazines, entropy — 28
shoegaze — 29
tofu — 30
learning — 31
your snow — 32
bang! and then — 33
budding — 34
seventh floor, crow — 35
kill all men club — 36
funeral — 37
St Tropez — 38
Charlie — 39
rituel — 40
licking future doctors — 41
l'Agonie — 42
in heaven — 43
Katharine — 44

web — 45
temples — 46
portrait of a girl in love… — 47
replacement service — 48
now is the winter — 49
futurology — 50
double denim — 51
three abduction fantasies — 52
acupuncture broadway — 54
patterns — 55
young adult — 56
lice — 57
fucked — 58
you envied the stars their height — 59
people change — 60
greek room — 61
paradise is for the blessed — 62
last laugh — 63
dream theory — 64
next life — 65
my small black shoes — 66
work — 67
the cloud — 69
push/phobias — 70
the stiff years — 71
crush — 73
thunder '14 — 74

Acknowledgements — 76

sick of the beats

there it is
but gorgeously
spat, wrung, never sets the sun
on the passenger's empire

garden garlanded
where the first men
played in Club Tropicana print –

which arm's underside? which theory
of forms – find me the demon
among the weeds,
pizza and Lucozade:

you, bitch of bad taste,
are vital to America
where someday only the sea
will remain!

what is ambition
if not inclusion
in the picture special?
a beat laid down
and paying to come, so beautiful

you'd tear apart
your tongue among
the finest minds of
(your generation – can't
and won't)

now the time, the night
to see the comet
with the horse's tail –

what is your medium?
you don't make a sound
even quietly.

destroy or otherwise, i find
we fall into categories –
those who do
and those who don't
notice the insect, suddenly.

what are you, opposite,
but we do not touch?
all the world
making dark selenium promises,
and yet, love –

wondering
what higher place it is
you walk in, where you sleep,

and how retain that
state of grace.

she's a star

remember brother.
heated pools, youth dismembered
in bright colloidal silver –

for lunch, honeydew melon.
holding it in her hands
like a slice of daybreak –

her nails bright important spikes.

you can put it anywhere

this work was conceived
as a reaction to vegetarianism
based on false hypotheses, intended
to raise awareness of the victims
of Great British Ketamine and Yoko
Ono jokes

primarily a work of protest
against the subpoena served
to Naomi Campbell and a shout out
to my boys – to be experienced
as shame and social castigation
consolidated and pushed in like a knife.

Humbert Summer

subtly dirtied
by four-day drinking in a basement flat
i feel like bunting, a paisley tie,
and private wasp stings
on a powder-blue day –

you're old,
you won't get it.

i want an epic landscape
sick of pushing syllables
down the stairwell   (ha–gi–o–graph–ic)
on some middle-class Beasley Street.

a callow retromaniac
i idolise violence and Duran Duran:
but i don't want either
to happen to me.

my first world problems:
intertextuality, shit MD,
and the inevitable death
of David Bowie.

indie

i cannot think of
a new form of closeness

that does not involve
the mutual ingestion of blood

glitch

you'll be blown down
by their belief in casting a purple shadow
which may seem crass or confrontational but
you sell your ass on the internet, what do you know?

they could be sisters
except they like each other:

one draws pentacles on Polaroids and the other looks like Cat Marnell.

Valerie Solanas

dis-cretion is the better part
of not an act -ress, insult riter
for a dime uncharacteristic
thirty-tu automatic, that
on the day she wore make-up

Billy says the whole
the sorry show made him
made Andy unlovable un
lovely as a slice of
peanut brittle spunked
snag-hag up the walls in hotels
Chelsea / Bristol / Bellevue
these traditional structures
– of Leonard Cohen songs abt fellatio
satin sheets in – th bourgeois   theatre

like last days all
pneumonic -matic misery

her mother burned her belongings posthumously

cat

the cat appeals –
barely containing viciousness in repose
blixblacks   chipped glass in the hands

like purple flowers – an important grave

zygote

'… here the female is hardly more than an abdomen, and her existence
is used up in the monstrous travail of ovulation.'
— Simone De Beauvoir

sheer-pink, inside a visible ruby,
smallshrimp, tiny, terrible.
scale: the bead of amber –
pendant for a pharaoh ant

neither pre- nor post- proletariat,
mouthless, but not unlike
Nico. soft pussycat
paralympian,
washing her hair
in the swamp of ages –

the clitorids

twisting in the bed sheets
like a string of plastic beads
clitorid – rose gold girl –

she's dreaming
perhaps about
her stomach being sliced open
by a dog with a knife

ars poetica

boy, you want to toss a while
in my dark and back-to-nature thoughts –
know that i am serially unkind
to those who love me
because i am young, have flame
in my skin and believe
that these people
exist in infinite supply –

my feelings sitting alone in a copy room at 1am,
and when looking at your face and when
remembering that coat
i lent

will seldom
constellate.

so smoke a joint in bed
and watch the mists of immortality
coagulate:

going down might earn you
at worst an anecdote in five years, at best

a footnote
in fifty.

autophilia

when the road is hot you've got
to take the power, my diamonds –
resolute as bone saw.

skin
on neoprene!
o, martini blue –
they scraped me off the moon.

letting it go, Boys of Summer
on the radio, hey bitch! This car
is a means to kill –
hopes and dreams
poised on the dash in conjunctive irony.

touch the leatherette my civic explosion, this shit
slow-motion, sliding the shard from my thigh –
sipping shakes and remembering good times

that splash of blood on my tennis skirt
and our pictures in the archive.

Joshua

sitting next to you on the bus even if you smelled of sex and hangovers –
you're the shit song stuck in my head, my bitter bitter little end but i never met
a Y chromosone with more to say and less will to say it with. The dank
has wrecked your faculties. let me bear you up on these gilded wings
while you make toast

every sun-split morning –

Rick James

Alprazolam – seems to me
a complicated way of saying
Xanax – whose primary use
is the treatment of anxiety disorder,
that said, it is
the most misused benzodiazepine
available on the US market.

Diazepam and bupropion, the white
sisters of hypnotism – a benefit of the former
being rapid onset action. Citalopram
has been know to cause genital anaesthesia,
a tragic localisation. Hydrocodone –
semi-synthetic, a droplet on a leaf.

Digoxin is an extract
of the *Digitalis*, instrument of
fairy thunder, bells of dead men,
threat-flower. Chlorphenamine
is a known performance enhancer,
used by the ancient Greeks
to help them run mazes faster.

Methamphetamine may need
no further introduction, kiss curl
drooping over an abject
2D structure, like cocaine
and associated man- euph-
oria, in 1919 crystallised
by Akira.

none were present in the bloodstream
of James Ambrose Johnson Jr.
in sufficient quantities to pose

a threat to life in and of
themselves, though in orchestra

they made a convincing explanation
for his prior behaviour.

fashion week

i bought the gladioli as a joke
obviously –

i don't see that it matters
that Pall Malls come in sets of twenty
when you've gone back to Lucky Strikes
and wearing the black bones of veneration
shamanistically.

mixtapes are a form
of autoeroticism

generated
in the absence of external stimuli
when you don't have a girlfriend
and *just happen* to like Morrissey.

hate

she believes the earth 'laughs through flowers'
and other asinine things

i know her pretty well
by now

but it *still gets me every time*

Ross and Rachel as invertebrates

the vacillations
of their on-off love affair
hold us rapt –

like the soft undulations
of their lilac swimmerets.

magazines, entropy

this is ageing i suppose
this thin
covering of moss and
particles
a good day is one in which
i plan
an outfit and
all those glass jars
rinsed out and saved
are thick
as milk mangroves
with liquid food
for the lilies
and pointless
astromeia –
avocado stones
and the eggs
that houseflies lay –
it looks like coconut water.

i think i am developing
a visual currency
of boredom
all the low-hanging birds
and empty cans
and postcards

falling off the wall

and this is it
the end it must be
but at least there was some tenderness along the way.

shoegaze

poor thing
overtly posed
in a pea-coat,

bisecting the ashes
with the side of his boot:

Curtis lonely.

fuck you.
it still amuses me.

tofu

the bean-curd claims
it is *firm & silken*

but i don't like to eat things
so coyly insinuating

learning

the position of the right:
society as whole, organic body
threatened by the other, without
(cf. the burning of witches)

the position of the left:
society is disparate, and under
constant threat, from within
(cf. purges)

your conclusion:
the position of the left, is right.

your snow

it's so brittle
and the last leaf is shaped like a woman
folding her arms –

the days white frames
for desperate kissing

lost – argonaut
of bigger skies –

and clouds gloss:

those big slow lambs
have eaten mistletoe.

bang! and then –

scissors
white rice
beans
passport
radio, crank or solar powered
sterile gauze and wipes,
for personal sanitation –

a moment to reflect
on the iniquity of possession,

then you run.

budding

the girls are all *budding* –

staring at themselves in hell's mirrored ceiling,
faces bathed in hydroponic glow

the only things awake to the silence
beyond the south circular

seventh floor, crow

who approves of the crows' work –
their black disregard for architecture?

they are proper dead-eyed dangerous
like making the bed, then fucking a stranger.

kill all men club

for ms. e. griffiths

profanity pup, all
gossamer motivations:

be the bitch
that bleeds velvet!
we're *dignity*
in your double
bed.

someday
they'll find us prone

in pearls
and mother-perfume,
one filthy fur
between us

borrow a dress
and Dickinson's dashes,
rip it up

and start again.

history you know
feels like nothing
as it passes

and a man has got
to add up to –

funeral

tonight i attended
our joint funeral:

together, dead shy
among the thankless flowers,
we are, at least, adorable.

i wake at one to find
the distance between us
almost-gold, inviolable –

St Tropez

everything is older and further away.
George is in New York
reading my poetry exactly
as i intended it to be read.
love

nothing more than something
the cicadas blunt their heads on –
raspberries and boats,
pantomiming pain on a swing seat

thou-shalt-do-good, we spit
but do not rinse. i have no sense
for you today – just arrangements.

i try
but find there is only space
and time between us

an electric fence to keep the animals at bay.

Charlie

a séance with a true spirit of romance; Byron perhaps,
one club foot in the grave his ripped woollens sodden
with earth and syphilis – our gods turn away;
they will not accept your noontide sacrifice
of quail's eggs and soda bread. this is what you wanted all along
eros-stink, the darkness of the forest by the motorway
to be high as lilacs on our college walls and with *hell* scrawled
on bared chest to writhe like frost round the railings at night
starving for abandonment the communion dress
all torn to waif by apple-moths – eat mummy-powders
for the ache of what it is; our heads shaved to tatters –

pretend it is midnight and we are in a meadow.

i turn it in to songs to pass Saharan time
before you are an old and wet-lip man. until then,
it is always thursday – we have no plan –
and so that youth might thoroughly be thought
true paradise –

let us carry age   *a snake*
in us all.

rituel

be it known i bloom in winter –
regain my self-esteem

when love's symbols choke on knot and bug
and the mornings are rich
with September's blackened seed.

hold still in my mind
while i valourise you –

wonder what was made in those minutes
before the sound came back
to smother it,

the cigarette end dropped
and empty glass
collected up.

don't be afraid.
i'll micro-fashion –
we're like the children

nannied through Bedford Square:
pretending to be real people,

sometimes
even dressed like them.

licking future doctors

there is a photograph of that night,
when it seemed there were endless permutations
and possibilities

and the hand of the medical student
was on your knee. funny
to think he might push those fingers
into the bunched silk of entrails.

his eyes lasted in the dark
he was *beautiful*
you are an animal –

your instinct was to eat him.

l'Agonie

commenting on his friendship with Baudelaire,
Felicien notes
a mutual love of skeletons:
a crude line drawing of St Theresa
in a state of holy *déshabillé*,
receiving cunnilingus from a skull.
the Japanese call it *Ukiyo − e*,
the pressure of the bone within.
obtain a time-piece, strangle the hour,
swing from life's photogenic chandelier!

in heaven

our entry
was due to clerical error.

we find there is nothing to do
but fuck quietly in his frosted beard
you, man-moth
with a jaundiced wing.

sometimes he takes us in his hands and
his whispers dishevel our hair

you, boy, his tiger-lily,
and I his turtle dove.

what's not to love
when all time is spare time?
no deliverance
from the cold gun

just you and me in white
and the pain of being pure at heart.

Katharine

there was never
the tolling of bells,
just a sinking
on the stairs.

why, wherever
you were (a ward, not
unkind word)
did you not
say

'I cannot die, because I don't know how to.'

parts of me
still reeling from Heaney –
noli timere.
i saw them too,

the blackberries
by the motorway.
i sleep in the urge
to uncover and eat them.

it turned
on a new world
of radio play,
and there's the grief –
when love is an ether.

i could not find it in myself
to be cruel. for some time
i made,

but not what i meant to.

web

half past four
in the morning but
the air is still dark
and close

and arriving home
to a web in the doorframe
and spectral
threat of rain:

a wasp, half-live and
a spider strokes across

a fly – glaze –
green

and still struggling

temples

Mithras –
white ground
ghost is white in silent catnaps

spider-traps!
all icons
of evil

expand to fit
the space
available –

is *history or
the city*

Janus, ambidex?

portrait of a girl in love as an elephant from a Dalí painting

i sway
with one leg on either side of the river.
sometimes they shout up from the highest windows

ask me if it gets lonely here
where thin rainclouds touch
my thighs:

i tell them no –
i may be vast
and great

and grey as altars
but i have my love
my little love

whose heart must be great
to love me.

replacement service

blithe on the axis of snow burst fur coat cigarette smoke:
Archway turned muscovite with seagull puff n sleaze
my markless boy
asking who drags

this sudden knife of white –
who planned this intrusion
of the world beyond the given?

now is the winter

and so it is – cold, antifragile, divested as a spoon:
pebbledashing on midlands crematoria,
the spurious phrase, born breach in the witches cave –
it came out blue and crying in the north,
by every fountain and in every tiled concourse:
that there will always be a little space
and a scrap of screaming moor
for the boy and his enchanted bird,
the footless king of love and law.

futurology

fear of open spaces
has become endemic:

our heads are large
and pulse with light.

heroes of
the old-world

are encased
in blocks of perspex —

facilitating the emergence
of a critical discourse

apropos.
the poetry of their terminal shapes.

double denim

allow them to wash over you,
her sequences,   the sky pink as old hands

Pepto-Bismol –

it's almost comforting to know
that the colours

are the first thing
you will fail to recall

three abduction fantasies

I.
a blonde retrospectively
transfigured by female desire

the home-intruder: a classic of the genre –

an experiment in the inherent romance
of being loved so much

you are handcuffed to a radiator.

II.
the second represents
heresy with an inarguable (inevitable?)
resemblance to Jesus

and prison tattoos – tears for murder –

in a forest and
torn leather jacket

he'll make you feel like a child again:

naked and shaking –
down in the bright and blood-red leaves.

III.
the plush coverlet
of a motel bed and dollars wadded thick
as russian novels –

the boy is beautiful, with his bones
nearly visible: .

the heart neatly punctured
by the sadness of his china-blues
that refract that desperate sunset back at you –

just kids who couldn't bear the weight of the world.

that night at the station
you drink black coffee

and spit impressively in the face
of a law-enforcement officer.

acupuncture broadway

this street is filiform –
the big one is *Ganymede* and the little one *Europa*,
touched to the twisted scratch of blue, the meridians
under the skin

patterns

I.
every morning and without screaming, in yellow habit
birds wit and champion the Guiltless Waking, threaded on temperate radar
and the drear wing of summer rain – do you remember the dream? of going
back to blue eyes… *beautiful, he's the best fuck in the business.*

this is why i'm not allowed nice things –
and more's the pity that the body of a boy like a country will not commit
to memory further than the smell of city, a soft grey t-shirt and
          well-formed mouth –
of course, these were the *always,*

the parts that killed and touched you most.

II.
buy the milk. make the bed. knowing where to find and how best
hurt each other – it's what grown-ups do –

it's how your parents met. forget
the cemetery, and all the red beatitude of sun cracking the ice in his heart
as if on floating pains of lead – it was joy, but never unalloyed – sending nudes
in tiny games and variations

of bloody murder. just the same
these feelings feed on death in as much as death means

the *re-ordering of personality*, the correction
of what seemed defective anyway –   55

young adult

maybe five gin & tonics
a spliff in the garden
then the train back to Deptford –
only eight minutes
under elephantitis cloud.

with accidental recourse
to an occult racism
you could say it looked like something
third world

              the rags ripped
in scorched tongues of wind, the teenagers
abusing playground furniture.

lice

an obligate ecto
coot

nit snugged
head to head

two sisters
were shaved

to nib the
dreamy bleed

and a bigger boy
tied me

with a
skipping rope

to the
cherry tree.

fucked

this is one for the girls
who have lain a short way
off

while his body cools like a cinder
and felt part of nothing

just fucked

you envied the stars their height

the day folded:
like a cabbage white closing its wings
on a windowsill.

with the old worn-out risk,
the unexplainable, skewed
trigonometry
of drunkenness

you climbed the fire escape

got on the roof.
but once you were there, you
envied the stars

their height

and could not get back down.

★

people change –

my head swims
in the shower.

Bastard,
so clean
so wild!

i'd have you touch me
like an old thinker

invert me:
stand between my body

and delicious summer.

greek room

a marble torso four-times the size of mine:

better to imagine they were done
to scale

and dream enslavement
to this race

of huge and languid men —

paradise is for the blessed

imagine me this moonlight skank
high in bed discussing funeral songs or
the gorgeous narcissism of Eartha Kitt
feeling good
creative!

this is my love
my Osho

my way of saying sorry that
i never make you breakfast anymore.

last laugh

on the balcony that afternoon,

i suppose you had the last laugh when you pointed out the sky had
made a mouth
that looked like it was glistening with honey

and said i had *the glow of health* about me.

dream theory

I.
every dream i described to you was already immanent within
the language – death as an old house, picture frames
luminised
by dust, and outside, just long grass.

II.
i never wanted the floating babies with their slow blue limbs
and upside-down faces: excuse my subconscious. the
meaning
is obvious. wake up with the words

> *Christ was a man like any other*
>   *and was probably beautiful, too…*

III.
it's quiet where you are and i suppose i am waiting. dreams
of hair shows and a little Siamese. i was crying – but only
the captivity of the animals

could upset you my darling -

IV.
there's wisteria sprawled across your walls, oil and bees –
false-gold fur,
aureate collar, tanning in the garden.

only a single season in the bone-house – and not one of us

who isn't sorry.

next life

as though you and i were pieced together from among the things
of huge sublimity, always strung on bone or rigged by vein
irradiant and *ill* –

until the bitter end when they'd have us shed our skin
and sodium, fall out of love with flesh
and bruising in the warmth of amniotic beams

like sunlight falling in the window across your chest
and the white striped bowl of
ripe black cherries –

★

my small black shoes
in the hallway –

and heart held

in his mouth

work

I.
it was a young woman who tended this garden
and there you are – cut glass!
product – the weak have none.

i stripped for you, emptied the ash tray
wondering why

you'd made this a dissection chamber.
all quiet insinuating light, hanging masks,
red fruit on the kitchen table

and your obvious joke of a car

outside –

II.
as British citizens it is our legal responsibility
to obscure these such acts

to the utmost
of our ability.

(still naked) *You said i had to monetise*
my talents

> (which are many – you'd know if you'd asked me
to describe the ways in which you disgust me) *no lust in this coma,*
> *even for a fifty -*

but then again
you're giving me two-hundred

baby

III.
nothing beats the dry hour sitting
on the side of the bath and wondering what you even are
'these days'

thinking   *I care a lot about me and I want to be happy*

★

the cloud
is a yellow sun-dress
floating on cold, superb water –

someday we'll live
somewhere warm
together.

push / phobias

ept. es. in coral and profile
my four-sleeper —

makes me queen of turning ·
my face away in sadness — at the funeral they say
the family took centre stage

and moths
crepe, crepe-eating
to you they're all cadaver.

this
the central drama:

and there it goes — do we fall
into each other as in
to mothers?

i am brave
while the ceiling beats with your terror —

the stiff years

I.
consider the rain: the beginning
and numbing prolongation –
everyone is lonely
and has regrets they live by

and yet the ivy that slides in the third-floor window
is heavy like boys' eyelashes –
could have roots
in the invention of love –

my dear
you made me kick a mirror.

my left foot bled profusely
and i wondered how it was that killers
ever get things clean again.

II.
a dream where the seamstress in lilac astrakhan
shoots a rapist in the head
with a cattle-gun.

a sunken church filled with statues
from the Vatican
and my subconscious is
for the main part carnage and internal rhyme.

i can never get back to the pleasant ones, just the ones where

the body is dropped naked into a soft black bank
of pine-needles and the heat
of the southern, unknown forest –

my dear, my darling, do you hear me where you sleep?

III.
a lovely thought
to take you where there's sea-aster.

that kind of peace where the sky is cold, impolitic –
when it is silent except that i hear our footsteps

and the breath that is coming from your body
that warm breath and body clutching hard at oxygen

as if it had hurt you
or done something wrong

and have nothing to say – nothing to say.

crush

first a thermosphere and the puddles are like melted chrysolite –
the world loves a coward with gambling debts and his own blood
    on his jeans.

you must breathe – always - if only out of deference to me.
    like the death
of a thousand white horses –

even when below you i'll come quietly.

for all your faults
you're wild grass to me.

thunder '14

a thunderstorm and all the dogs are barking a thunderstorm and
you come back to me your glass-eyes full a portion a portion of
you for the gods and i say i think i believe in magic now: nature
likes to remind us sometimes / i will take on my nature
or flying rise to meet it / all so full like a velvet bag my belly a
black dress too short doesn't reach the floor but still there's a
drama in it / there you are singing *Yesterday* i'm pregnant by the
thunder god / infected by mythos Patti Stevie St Marie /
don't laugh / never laugh at me / you say you care you say you'll
kill him scale Olympus or his wide mid-western skies and take
the moon among your freckles / orange and blue and blue stars
that made this / that made you / so loud the thunder
i thought the streets would smash and we'd wake to craters
criminal mouths agape like the clouds had dropped to the Xerxe /
dropped like Leda from heights of infamy
to the rusting dogs and unsanctioned treetops / the way things
are in attitudes
of mutiny / and thunderbolts on in your ears like crazy horse
who vaults the skies
and his fringe of light tears at the signals and radio antenna /
chaos kaos rain
so heavy the only time she'd heard it like this before was in dream
where she was raped / or on a holiday in Hawaii / and the sky and
thunder say yes / yes, instant-
ly.

Acknowledgements

'Humbert Summer' and 'ars poetica' originally appeared in *Rising* zine.

'you envied the stars their height' was a winning poem in the 2008 Foyle Young Po ets of the Year competition, and was published in the anthology of winning poems.

'l'Agonie', 'dirty girls' and 'turkey neck' were published online by *clinic*.

'zygote', 'the clitorids' and 'fucked' were published in *Cuntry Living* zine.

'hate' and 'replacement service' were published in *Hypersanity* zine.

'b. 1991' and 'now is the winter' were published online by *Morning Star*.

'Katharine' was originally published in *Swimmers* zine.

'in heaven' was published by *Isis* magazine.

'Joshua', 'patterns' and 'next life' were published in *Poetry London*.

'licking future doctors' was first published in *Brittle Star*.

'in heaven', 'Charlie', 'you envied the stars their height', 'portrait of a girl in love as an elephant from a Dalí painting' and 'sunflowers' all appeared in earlier form in a pamphlet released as part of Nasty Little Press's *Nasty Little Intros* series.

Thank you to Dad, Katrina, Kezia, George, Elle and James – also to Clare Pollard and Tim Wells, the Poetry Society, Emily Berry and the editors of the publications in which these poems originally appeared.

⬡⬡ EYEWEAR PUBLISHING

EYEWEAR POETRY

MORGAN HARLOW MIDWEST RITUAL BURNING
KATE NOAKES CAPE TOWN
RICHARD LAMBERT NIGHT JOURNEY
SIMON JARVIS EIGHTEEN POEMS
ELSPETH SMITH DANGEROUS CAKES
CALEB KLACES BOTTLED AIR
GEORGE ELLIOTT CLARKE ILLICIT SONNETS
HANS VAN DE WAARSENBURG THE PAST IS NEVER DEAD
DAVID SHOOK OUR OBSIDIAN TONGUES
BARBARA MARSH TO THE BONEYARD
MARIELA GRIFFOR THE PSYCHIATRIST
DON SHARE UNION
SHEILA HILLIER HOTEL MOONMILK
FLOYD SKLOOT CLOSE READING
PENNY BOXALL SHIP OF THE LINE
MANDY KAHN MATH, HEAVEN, TIME
MARION MCCREADY TREE LANGUAGE
RUFO QUINTAVALLE WEATHER DERIVATIVES
SJ FOWLER THE ROTTWEILER'S GUIDE TO THE DOG OWNER
TEDI LÓPEZ MILLS DEATH ON RUA AUGUSTA
AGNIESZKA STUDZINSKA WHAT THINGS ARE
JEMMA BORG THE ILLUMINATED WORLD
KEIRAN GODDARD FOR THE CHORUS
COLETTE SENSIER SKINLESS
BENNO BARNARD A PUBLIC WOMAN
ANDREW SHIELDS THOMAS HARDY LISTENS TO LOUIS ARMSTRONG
JAN OWEN THE OFFHAND ANGEL
A.K. BLAKEMORE HUMBERT SUMMER
SEAN SINGER HONEY & SMOKE
RUTH STACEY QUEEN, JEWEL, MISTRESS

EYEWEAR PROSE

SUMIA SUKKAR THE BOY FROM ALEPPO WHO PAINTED THE WAR
ALFRED CORN MIRANDA'S BOOK

EYEWEAR LITERARY CRITICISM

MARK FORD THIS DIALOGUE OF ONE - WINNER OF THE 2015 PEGASUS AWARD
FOR POETRY CRITICISM FROM THE POETRY FOUNDATION (CHICAGO, USA).